Contents

Published by Oak Tree Press, Cork T12 EVT0, Ireland
www.oaktreepress.com / www.SuccessStore.com

ISBN: 978-1-78119-428-7 (Paperback)
ISBN: 978-1-78119-340-2 (ePub)
ISBN: 978-1-78119-341-9 (Kindle)
ISBN: 978-1-78119-342-6 (PDF)

A catalogue record of this book is available from the British Library.

Brain Images by Phillip Cullen

Foreword

As Professor of Psychology at Trinity College Dublin and the Founding Director of the Institute of Neuroscience Trinity College, Dublin, I co-supervised Celine while she was a PhD student. Celine was always an ambitious and independent thinker. Her work since then - and some of it now available to you, the reader, in the **Maximising Brain Potential** series - is no different.

In this first book, Celine draws on newly-published knowledge about the brain's role in habit to explain the complexities of the brain in the learning and habit change process. Her ability to translate this complex science into easy-to-understand prose means that readers of all backgrounds will be able to grasp the brain's role in making changes and learn how to implement these changes for themselves. This book is also well-suited for those at management levels who want to make learning a priority for their staff.

I can think of no one more qualified to write this book, as Celine has been putting the theories in this book into practice in her work for many years with the company she founded: Adaptas, a learning and development business through which Celine has successfully coached and facilitated learning in thousands of leaders and teams worldwide – from Ireland and the UK, to North America, to Africa. Her form of training is unique and receives exceptional reviews, with many people saying they wished they had learned this information "10 years previously". Her clients deliver overwhelmingly positive reviews, expressing appreciation for Celine's ability to "create a safe space" and create "amazing outcomes".

With this book, Celine brings to the reader the science and theory that drives her successful training. Celine's insights should not be overlooked.

Professor Ian Robertson - Clinical Psychologist and Neuroscientist, Author of *The Stress Test: How Pressure Can Make You Stronger and Sharper; The Winner Effect: The Science of Success and How To Use It; Mind Sculpture: Your Brain's Untapped Potential; The Mind's Eye: An Essential Guide to Boosting Your Mental Power.*

The only skill that will be important in the 21st century is the skill of learning new skills. Everything else will become obsolete over time.

Peter Drucker [1]

A Note From The Author

As a psychologist and coach working in organisations worldwide and with individuals, groups and teams, I have noticed over the past 10 years plus that very few new discoveries from neuroscience are being integrated into education, learning and development or soft skills programmes. As someone who works to help people maximise their potential in a range of organisations and educational institutions, I believe that many eager and dedicated people are missing out on vital tools for life and leadership.

Enough is enough. So much money is being spent on soft skills education in organisations. Yes, it is wonderful that decision-makers have recognised the value and importance of learning for success. But the problem is that most people attend great courses, workshops, programmes and then nothing or very little changes in their behaviour. There are many reasons for this that might surprise you and that are covered in this short book. Time and time again, in recent years I see the difference that knowing this information makes to a person's commitment to change and to their own long-term behavioural change.

Reading this book will help you to see learning from a new perspective. Awareness of the concepts in this book will help you to open up to learning new things and enable you to maintain the elements that make long-term behavioural change possible.

How do I know this works?

With my clients over the years, I have learned by observing what is effective and what is not in creating change. People who have taken on this information have made long-term behavioural change, while those who have not taken it on board have not had the same success.

This book is the first in the **Maximising Brain Potential** series. The **Maximising Brain Potential** series is based on the most up-to-date scientific research of how our brain potential can be maximised for habit change, learning, productivity and health. This series of books pulls this information together into digestible chunks. The others in the series include **Developing Learning Addicts: The 7 Steps to Learning & Habit Change** and **Change Begins Here: Building The Foundations for Learning & Habit Change**. These books both introduce additional concepts and also probe deeper into some of the topics discussed in this book.

Similar to the current wave of just-in-time learning, where learning is available on-demand, and can be accessed when the learner needs it, the **Maximising Brain Potential** series of books is just-what-you-need-to-know-to-make learning-easier in adulthood.

I know that this text will be useful for you, whether you want to make a change in your own life, or you are involved in helping others learn and make change. If you would like more, we also have workshops and an online course available to help guide you through a process to maximise your brain potential.

Contact **info@adaptastraining.com** for information.

Dr. Celine Mullins, Adaptas

Acknowledgements

This may be a short book but it takes a long time and a lot of people to create something that has real clarity and actually gets to the point of publication!

Without the assistance of Diana Friedman and Enda Hughes, this text would not make half as much sense as it does now. Their patient reading, editing, re-reading, and editing, as well as encouragement and advice, is hugely appreciated. The process has taught me much about how writing is re-writing and re-writing is writing!

Thank you to Eve Johnston, John Mulreid, Laura McCarthy and Ciara Byrne for reading, suggestions and ongoing encouragement and belief.

Thank you to Brian at Oak Tree Press for seeing the potential, and for patience with each 'near final draft' email!

Thank you to Agne Vabamäe for pulling together so much of the information I had written over the course of a number of years and creating a beautiful first version of this book.

Thank you also to Camille Donegan, Claire Comerford, Alistair McBride, Paul O'Kelly and Padraig and Angela Mullins for ongoing encouragement.

Thank you to Annie Keeney for patient checking of references and footnotes.

Thank you to Regina Heffernan and Catriona Walsh, who read an early draft and expressed enthusiasm that drove me forward. And to Dr. Richard Roche for painstakingly being my second pair of eyes with the neuroscience!

Thank you to Claire Comerford and Enda Hughes for pushing me out of my comfort zone and encouraging me to do more with this text, beyond my original plans.

Thank you also to Sinead Kennedy, Eve Bulman and Niamh Ni Dhonaill, whose encouragement did not go unnoticed!

And a final thank you to my clients. I share some examples of clients I have worked with but have changed some names and small details to protect their anonymity.

Why Read This Book?

This book will:

1. Help you to **use your brain more effectively** when learning new skills, by offering simple and practical tips.

2. Support you in **breaking old habits and creating new ones**.

3. Give you great insights into **organisational learning and development**-related topics that you can use in your organisation

The illiterate of the 21st century will not be those who cannot read and write, but those who cannot learn, unlearn and relearn.

Alvin Toffler [2]

Introduction

Are you a leader who recognises that learning is one of the main keys to business success? Are you working in a Learning & Development or Talent Management role? Are you trying to change habits to be more successful at work or to live a healthier life? If any of these traits or roles describe you, then you have come to the right place.

We all recognise the speed of change that is happening around us. Our working roles will look dramatically different in the very near future. For example, due to the elements of the working day that are being replaced by Artificial Intelligence, it is predicted that many of us will need to retrain perhaps many times in our lifetime. Keeping our brain functioning properly and performing efficiently is worth some serious thought. The period of accelerated change we are living through at the moment requires higher levels of learning agility than ever seen before. We will all have a lot of learning to do throughout our adult working lives.

Some of us are naturally motivated to learn and change how we do things. But for many of us, initial motivation is only short-lived. Children soak up learning from the people and environment they are surrounded by. You will probably have already recognised that learning doesn't feel quite as simple as when you were a child. Why? Because by the time you reach adulthood, much of your behaviour consists of habits. These habits allow your brain to conserve energy, but also make learning a challenge.

In recent years, scientists have made many exciting and ground-breaking discoveries on how the brain learns and changes throughout adulthood. However, much of this recent research from neuroscience, physiology, psychology and more is not being implemented into how we learn as adults. This book seeks to change that.

As you will see in this book, your brain changes throughout adulthood and must be consciously harnessed in the direction you wish. The perspective on how our brain functions covered in this book forms the very basis of how we can best learn and, in my opinion, needs to be at the foundation of all learning. The purpose of this book is to help support your learning journey and the learning journey of those around you.

Briefly, there are three main elements to consider:

1. Adult learning is habit change and **old habits die hard**.

2. Understanding how our brain functions is a vital tool for learning.

3. The brain is focused on energy saving **and that energy saving blocks us from doing things differently**.

Adult Learning is Habit Change

'Learning' and 'habit change' are inextricably linked. You have lots of habitual routines that block you from replacing older ways of operating. People seldom consider the connection between habit and learning when they wish to make a change in their own life or in helping others learn and make change. But when you are learning something new, you need to keep the brain focused and you need to repeat new actions to overcome old ways of doing things – habits. Otherwise, long-term behavioural change does not occur. Chapter 1 explains this important relationship between learning and habit change.

Understanding How our Brain Functions is a Vital Tool for Learning

Having an understanding and mental picture of how our brain is functioning is in itself a vital tool to allow you to make changes in the brain because it gives you a sense of perspective. It allows you to feel like you are stepping outside of yourself and seeing what is happening inside the 'control centres' of the brain. The very fact that you are now reading this book and embarking on seeing the brain in your mind's eye means you are already visualising learning differently. Chapter 2 will assist you with this process.

The Brain is Focused on Energy Saving

The area of the brain that creates automatic behaviours is your greatest friend - but also your greatest foe. Our brain creates habits to let us go about our days, doing much of what we do automatically and with little thought. This saves brain energy and frees up your brain for other important tasks like logical analysis. The problem comes when we try to learn something new, as older information and habits are embedded. These habits take some effort to undo! Adults have less time and often less energy than children, and so adult learning requires a lot more conscious effort than childhood learning. Chapter 2, as well as helping you understand how your brain functions in learning and habit change, also explains how the biological drive for self-protection can hinder your learning.

The objective of this book is not just to give you an understanding of the brain, learning and habit change. The objective is to activate that understanding as a fundamental mechanism to learning. And therefore, Chapter 3 provides you with strategies to help make learning happen in a much more effective way, by overcoming the brain's self-protection mode.

CHAPTER ONE:

The Important Relationship Between Adult Learning and Habit Change

Kay's Story

Kay had recently won a promotion. She was now line manager to four people. Each of these four were managing two or three people each. When I met Kay, she appeared slightly reserved, or perhaps shy or lacking in confidence. She had been offered some coaching with me on moving into this new role. On our first meeting I sat with her and her own line manager to discuss objectives for the coaching. I noticed that Kay's manager did most of the talking, explaining why Kay had been offered coaching. There were no concerns around Kay's operational expertise, she was clearly excellent at what she did. Her line managers concern was that at this level Kay had moved into, there would be more challenges around managing people. She would have more people reporting to her and she would also have more reporting responsibilities to other key stakeholders in the business, both external and internal.

Kays line manager had a few main observations. Firstly, Kay would need to collate the information she was gathering from stakeholder to present to senior management in a more concise and clear manner. Secondly, Kay would have to delegate more effectively to her team. Thirdly, she said that Kay appeared to spend most meetings making notes rather than engaging fully in the conversation. She insisted that Kay would need to find a way to look like she was more engaged through body language, more eye contact, less note taking, if she was going to be effective as an influencer of the various stakeholders.

When I eventually interrupted Kay's line manager to ask Kay what she would like to get out of working with me as a coach, Kay repeated back what her own line manager had said in slightly different words. And indeed, I noticed that she appeared to have great respect for her own line manager, perhaps potentially bordering on disquiet.

When I eventually got Kay on my own when her manager left us to it, I explained to Kay that I always find that people get more out of coaching when they get really clear on what they personally want and why they want it. As our conversation progressed, it was clear that Kay was lacking in confidence and was very concerned she would fail. She had attended a leadership development programme the previous year in the run up to this promotion, and when she interviewed for the new role, she convinced herself that she has done a terrible job in the interview and would not get the role. So, she was delighted when she was told she had got the role. She believed ultimately that this new role was suited better to her knowledge and experience. She was more interested in this side of the business than the department she had previously worked. However, there was a real fear of failure.

I asked her what she could recall from the leadership programme she had completed. She said the facilitator was very nice. I asked her again what she could recall, and she said there had been some interesting information about communication and influencing, and a good module on strategic thinking. I asked her in what ways she had applied what she had learned on this programme. She told me that once she had got back to work, things were so busy after missing two days out of the business; that she had to park it all and get back into the day-to-day work.

This is something I hear all the time, so I was not surprised. I shared with Kay that I hoped this experience would be different and that a big part of our work together would involve going back to work and applying as much as she could from what we covered and that there would be homework between our meetings, including reflective writing to help her embed the learnings.

I also shared with her some information about how the brain learns, what is required to create long lasting behavioural change and promised I would send her on some extra information to read on this before we next met.

We spent some time digging into what she wanted to get from coaching. It turned out I was on to something with the line manager. It became clear that she was fearful, on a daily basis, of doing something wrong in this new role and that her line manager would be displeased. So, I knew we would need to do some work on this fear if Kay was going to make the changes she needed to and if she wanted to make the most of this new role and enjoy her new responsibilities to the full. We agreed some plans to get there and agreed on some homework exercises to help her dig into this fear.

In my experience, many of us have a fear of something. Not just spiders, or heights. But many of us have deeply held beliefs that others will think we are stupid if we say the wrong thing, or fears that we will let other people down, and they will be disappointed in us and that will have a negative impact. Many of us have a fear of being humiliated in front of our colleagues or think that we will be found out, that we are not truly capable of fulfilling the role we have been hired for or promoted to.

In my work as a coach and facilitator of personal change and growth, I notice that sometimes people are conscious of these fears, and do not know what to do about them. I also notice that others are not conscious at all of these fears and do not realise how these deeply held fears are sabotaging them.

I personally have transformed my own behaviour many times over the years, around for example, my confidence. I had to deal with some big fears when I set up my own business and started working with groups and teams. And even, quite recently, I've had to look deeper at some of my own fears in making some changes to my business model and keeping me stuck in old habitual ways of being.

As you read on, regardless of which camp you are in, it will start making sense to you why I thought it important to bring this information together. If you, like me and countless others I have worked with, have been to a workshop, been on a leadership development programme, gone through coaching, listened to a podcast, read a book and can honestly say you have changed very little or not enough, the information here will hopefully explain all.

What is Learning?

Learning is the acquisition of knowledge or skills through study, experience, or being taught.

Until recent advances in technology, investigation of the brain was only possible posthumously and in animals. We could not investigate the 'living' human brain and so we could only make guesses as to what was happening in there. Due to progress made in the fields of physiology, neuroscience and more, we have started getting a clearer picture of what is happening inside the brain. Researchers have been able to go inside the 'living' brain and observe how learning actually occurs at the molecular level. Additionally, more sophisticated experiments with the brains of laboratory animals are stretching the bounds of our understanding further. Of course, the human brain and the behaviour it supports is far more complex than that of other species. However, relevance of research is aided by considerable cross-species similarities in behaviour and biology between humans and other mammalian species. And now, because of nanotechnology, computer technology, optical techniques and much more, it is possible to measure a number of cells at once and to create more extensive and richer animal models, from which to understand even the smallest actions.

We now know that the brain acts as a dense network of fibre pathways consisting of approximately 80 billion neurons. A neuron is a nerve cell that receives and sends electrical signals over long distances within the body. A neuron receives electrical input signals from sensory cells (called sensory neurons) and from other neurons. Each neuron is connected to thousands of others via links called synapses. These synapses can be strong or weak. A strong link indicates a significant influence between connecting neurons. A weak link could be thousands of times weaker than a strong one.

Neurons are important to understanding habit change and learning, because learning and memory formation occur by the strengthening and weakening of the synapses – that is, connections between these neurons. Researchers find that, when two neurons frequently interact, they form a bond that allows them to transmit signals more easily and accurately. This leads to more complete memories and easier recall. Conversely, when two neurons rarely interact, the transmission is often incomplete, leading to either a faulty memory or no memory at all.

This is why I explained to Kay that if she wanted to make real and lasting change, it was going to take a lot more than our coaching sessions and the previous leadership development programme with all it's great tips and tools. She was going to have to get to know herself better. She was going to have to get new neurons to communicate with each other.

Note: It's important to consider that our learning is also influenced by the feedback we receive, the sleep we get, the food we eat, and much more. More on these topics can be found in the two other books in the **Maximising Brain Potential** series. Should you wish to expand your knowledge and to learn further strategies beyond this book, you know where to find it.

What is a Habit?

Scientifically speaking, habits are a redundant set of automatic unconscious thoughts, behaviours, and emotions that are acquired through repetition and are acts we generally perform in the same way in the same situations. Or, to look at it in simpler terms, a habit can be defined as a settled or regular tendency, behaviour or practice.

Habits are part of being human. It is believed that more than 40% of our daily behaviours are habits. Because they are automatic, many of these habits help us to get through our day without having to think and waste energy. For example, brushing our teeth, having a shower, or embarking on our daily commute to school or work are all beneficial habits. Other habits that might not serve us well or keep us healthy include eating a pastry every morning as we rush to the office or hogging the couch for an evening or avoiding exercise for the third week in a row.

As we go through our days, we generally believe we are making moment-to-moment decisions, but many more of our behaviours are habits, more automatic than you might realise. Think about it this way; a habit is when you've done something so many times that your body knows how to do it better than your mind. And in many ways, this does serve a useful purpose. If we had to make new decisions every day, we would probably be exhausted before 9am!

At the same time, habits can also make our behaviours quite rigid; for example, many managers I work with operate using learned habits such as micromanaging or not providing sufficient feedback. Usually these are habits that they have picked up during their career or from their own managers. Typically, these habits are not conducive to creating happy, motivated people and high-performing teams. Habitual behaviour can also be detrimental in the workplace – for example, when we approach a new project the same way we've approached every other similar project, even though our customer needs a very different solution.

There are many habits we could create that would help us operate more effectively in work and life, yet many of us do not realise better habits are ours to learn.

Take Kay; she was used to communicating in a certain way. For decades she had taken notes in school and meetings. During her career to date, she had communicated information utilising data and excluding any type of examples or stories to influence stakeholders. For a long time, she had tried to manage and fix everything that her teams did incorrectly and had stopped delegating certain things. She's done a good job and she keeps getting promoted. Why would she do anything differently if it's worked so far for her?

The award-winning New York Times business reporter Charles Duhigg (2013)[3] tells us in his book *The Power of Habit* that habits serve an incredibly important evolutionary and survival function:

> *Habits emerge because the brain is constantly looking for ways to save effort. Left to its ow devices, the brain will try to make almost any routine into a habit because habits allow our minds to ramp down more often. This effort-saving instinct is a huge advantage – an efficient brain requires less room, which makes for a smaller head, which makes child birth easier, and therefore causes fewer infant and mother deaths. An efficient brain also allows us to stop thinking constantly about basic behaviours such as walking and choosing what to eat, so we can devote mental energy to inventing spears, irrigation systems and eventually airplanes and video games. But conserving mental effort is tricky because, if our brains power down at the wrong moment, we might fail to notice something important such as a predator hiding in the bushes or a speeding car as we pull on to the street, so our **basal ganglia** have devised a clever system to determine when to let habits take over.*

Later, we will take a closer look at the basal ganglia (a group of structures found deep within the cerebral hemisphere in the brain stem) because among its many purposes, it stores our habits.

Scientists in many different fields have been attracted to the study of habits because of the power habits have over behaviour and because they invoke a dichotomy between the conscious, voluntary control over behaviour, considered the essence of higher-order deliberative behavioural control, and lower-order behavioural control that is scarcely available to consciousness.

Ann Graybiel [4]

The brain converts the sequence of actions involved in performing an action, 'chunking' them to the primitive basal ganglia, reserving the cerebral cortex for higher or more intensive functions. Because of the great job the basal ganglia does of storing our habits and therefore making much of our behaviour automatic, we often fail to seek new ways of doing and seeing things. This is what often blocks our ability to learn new things.

Kay, even though she was open to learning, had struggled to behave differently in this new role so far, even though she was supposed to be stepping it up. In many ways this was because of her Basal Ganglia.

While we might believe that we can't or don't need to change our habits (and it does often feel this way as we have developed many of them over a lifetime), much research and experience shows that we can change if we want to. It just takes quite a bit more effort and conscious awareness as adults than it did when we were children. And Kay was yet another example of this. The day-to-day of life and work didn't enable her time to get specific enough on the change. Indeed, most of us don't work in environments where it feels safe to try things out and fail in order to start building the new habits.

So how do we go about changing some of our entrenched habits when it comes to learning and change? As we will discover, learning and habit change are inseparable.

The Relationship between Learning and Habit Change

Until recent decades, scientists believed that the brain was hard-wired by the time we hit adulthood. And this seemed to confirm why, as adults, we found it difficult to learn new things. Sayings like "you can't teach an old dog" became quite popular.

However, as mentioned, recent studies of the 'living' brain now show that the process of neurons forming bonds when new learning occurs continues throughout adulthood. Science shows us that regardless of age, it is possible for learning to occur and for us to change habits until the day we die.

In the act of learning, our brain solves problems and processes information. But it is not always obvious how our automatic behaviours that occur without conscious thougwht are controlling our actions when we are learning new ways to do things.

The difficulty for us as adult learners is that our habits are so engrained that they often get in the way of our learning.

For most of us, habit change is challenging. The reason for this is because we are often trying to change our habits 'in the dark'. We don't quite realise how so much of what we do is a whole lot of habits. For example, as mentioned Kay attended a leadership programme, which took place over six months and consisted of 6 modules on various topics, from strategic thinking to leading change to ethics and social responsibility. She arrived at the first day of the initial two-day module of the programme ready to learn and take it all back to work to apply. She was really looking forward to hearing from the teachers and experts about the various topics. She told me she enjoyed the two days and picked up some useful tips. After the two days, she returned to the office with her notes in tow and some good intentions of a few things she was going to do differently. One month later, on arriving to Module 2, she remembered that she had safely placed her notes in a folder but she hadn't got a chance to re-read the notes and she hadn't really had time to apply any of the take-away's from Module 1.

What happened? She attended two days of learning. Once she left, her habits took over. It wasn't enough that she attended the module and heard about some new concepts and approaches and had some great intentions. She didn't actually convert this new information to her brain and her actions. In effect she attended a learning event, but it did not impact on her behaviour.

Remember, a habit is when you've done something so many times that your body knows how to do it better than your mind. When we attend a course, our engrained habits will get in the way of implementing new learning. Kay is no different to any of us.

As an adult, you need to approach learning with a conscious plan for applying the new 'learning'. To apply the new knowledge will involve breaking the old habits and making a clear plan for holding yourself accountable to embedding the new ways of operating (or getting someone else to hold you accountable if you respond to that better). Creating the new habits to get the new learning to stick takes focus and repetition.

In adulthood, it is challenging to achieve all of this as the busy-ness of life gets in the way. And few of us view changing our habits as 'fun'. In the workplace, many people see learning and change as cause for frustration. We often see such activity as a struggle, boring, or too much effort and time-wasting. In particular, as we'll see later, our unconscious beliefs and our brain's automatic focus on protecting us from danger means that, if the brain could speak, it would tell us that it doesn't see changing our habits as fun or even as an option!

One of the challenging things with habits, and with operating as effectively as we might, is that everyone is different. All habits are different too. It would be great if we had a magic pill that could help us change the habits we wish to and clear space for the new learning, but it's not that simple. There is not just one single or simple way to change a habit. All of our habits are driven by different beliefs, by different cravings, by different emotions and require different strategies to address them. This is why the effort has to become more conscious. Changing how you operate involves getting to know yourself better!

For example, when I decided I wanted to feel more confident and impactful at making speeches or presentations, I needed different actions to change my habits, compared to when I decided I wanted to build healthier morning eating habits.

To become better at making speeches, I had to change how I did things in a number of ways, including how I prepared and delivered my presentation, and how I conquered my emotional reaction (fear) to public speaking. I had to study how to create content that was more interesting to my audience, which involved me really putting myself in their shoes, rather than just telling them what I thought they needed to hear. I had to say "Yes" every time I was asked to speak in public, even though it was terrifying for me and my mind screamed "NO". I had to retrain the limiting voices in my head. "What if I am not good enough". "what if I don't give the audience anything that's useful for them." I had to stand up and practice, practice, practice, even though it was much more appealing to spend my time doing other things - falling into old habits of just rehearsing a script in my head. You see? I had to learn new approaches, and I had to replace old habits with new habits and old beliefs with new beliefs.

On the other hand, to build better eating habits didn't require necessarily learning any new information but I had to change certain routines and get into the rhythm of performing a number of actions.

These included:

1. Planning ahead regarding what to purchase and what to make for meals.

2. Avoiding going grocery shopping on an empty stomach!

3. Making a vegetable juice or smoothie first thing in the morning to start my day a healthy way and set me up for a healthier start.

4. Getting out of bed 15 minutes earlier every morning to make the juice.

5. Not giving in to the 'snooze' button on my alarm, because this would get in the way of me having time to make the juice.

While these two approaches were different, there were a number of things these changes had in common as well. Both required changes to create the mindset and environment for the discipline to embed, to both learn new information, and to change old habits.

To start, I had to get clear on what I wanted to do differently and why. I had to learn some new concepts and approaches. In the case of the public speaking, I had to learn and apply daily mental exercises to change my habitual negative thought patterns. In the case of the morning juicing, I had to change both my morning and shopping routines.

In another example, when I decided to get better at having difficult conversations, I had to take yet another approach. First, I had to understand the stress response and learn a few difficult conversation structures. I then forced myself to have low-risk difficult conversations as often as possible. For example, I practiced with everyone from a bus driver (who was driving dangerously), to a gym instructor (who spent the whole class looking at himself in the mirror instead of checking if we were doing the exercises properly to avoid injury).

Changing our habitual routines starts with motivation to change. However, once the novelty and initial motivation disappears, the real key to change is ongoing discipline to ensure the repetition required to create the new habit. This discipline requires a plan, conscious effort and a lot of small actions on a daily basis to change the habits and embed the new approach.

Although embedding learning and habit change can be challenging in adulthood and can sometimes feel exhausting, putting a plan together to overcome the old ways and habits and then to embed the new learning and habits requires deciding on a number of small daily actions and then repeating them. In the next chapter, you will learn a little more about why conscious planning, action and repetition is so important, from the perspective of how the brain takes on new learning and in effect, how it changes as you learn.

Great things are not done by impulse, but by a series of small things brought together.

Vincent Van Gogh [5]

CHAPTER TWO:

Understanding The Power of the Brain and The Brain's Protection Mode

The Learning Brain

Because it is an organ built to learn, 'the brain' could be renamed 'the learning brain'. Recent research has shown that the brain has evolved to adapt and readapt to an ever-changing world. [7] In fact, the survival of our species is dependent on this ability of our brain to learn and change.

This ability is made possible by a process in the brain's chemistry and architecture called 'neuroplasticity'. Technically speaking, neuroplasticity is the ability of neurons to change their structure and relationships to one another in an experience-dependent manner according to environmental demands. [8,9]

For example, when rats are raised in a complex and challenging environment their brains grow. The size of the cortex, the length of neurons, the number of synapses, and the level of neurotransmitters and growth hormones all increase. [10,11,12,13,14]

However, the benefits of stimulating environments are not just reserved for the young.

When adult rats with early nervous system damage and genetically-based learning deficits are exposed to training and enriched environments (for example, interacting with a changing sensory and social environment; engaging in far more motor activity than regular caging), these more complex environments lead to enhanced cognitive and motor functions. [15,16,17,18,19]

Although it is not possible to do such invasive research with humans, much evidence suggests that our brains react in the same manner.[20]

This means that everything you think you know and feel now can change, depending on what you focus on. And that this capacity for learning and change is available to us throughout our entire lives.

Your brain - every brain - is a work in progress. It is 'plastic'. From the day we're born to the day we die, it continuously revises and remodels, improving or slowly declining, as a function of how we use it.

Michael Merzenich, 2013[6]

As mentioned earlier, the development of technology used to examine the brain has shown us that finding new ways of being and doing and avoiding habitual behaviours is more possible than we may have once thought.

So how do we do this? Building habits or changing existing ones generally involves weakening existing mature neural pathways that have been reinforced over years, by creating new neural pathways and using them until they are strengthened and become second nature.

This means being more conscious of the choices we are making. For example, if you have reached for the pastry every morning for years, the first day of changing this habit, you reach instead for an apple. By making this simple conscious choice, you begin the process of creating a new neural pathway. Each day you reach for the apple and not the pastry, the new pathway begins to get stronger and the old one weakens.

Let's take Kay as an example. She was managing a team and had been in the mode for years of giving solutions to her colleagues when they came with problems and were looking for help. This took up a lot of her time every day. She believed she was doing her role, managing and supporting her team. However, as we discussed this, she told me that if they interrupted her less, she would have more time to get what she needed done. The first time she changed this process by asking them what ideas they had, instead of giving them the quick solution, she began the process of creating a new neural pathway. Each time she asked them a question to help them come up with their own solution, the new pathway began to get stronger and the old one weakened. The same happened for her colleagues. Her colleagues got used to coming to her with some ideas and solutions to the problem, rather than just the problem. They eventually stopped interrupting her as much as they used to. She had empowered them to think about solutions for themselves. Their brains were in fact also changing.

With all learning, your brain is going through this process. By pushing yourself in a new way, your brain lays down new pathways and makes new neural connections.

Creating Supportive Habits

Hopefully, you can now understand that it is both possible and healthy to learn actively in adulthood, while at the same time there are many obstacles to us embedding our new learning. The brain is very happy to create new neural pathways, but we can sabotage the creation of those new pathways quickly.

What new skills do you wish to learn and what new habits do you desire to create?

You may have heard the 'rule' that it takes 21 days to change a habit.

But what often actually happens when we take on something like a 21-day challenge to change our behaviour? We generally give up as quickly as we started. Never mind 21 days; we usually stop after just a few days! It is so difficult for us to change a habit, and even the most committed, focused and disciplined of us struggle.

One key to getting rid of unwanted habits is to choose a new habit to replace the unwanted one. Repetition, exposure and emotional engagement with a new habit will strengthen the new pathway, over time. And eventually it becomes an easier path to take than your former habit.

Phillippa Lally and colleagues from the Cancer Research UK Health Behaviour Research Centre based at UCL Epidemiology and Public Health looked at how long it took people to reach a limit of self-reported automaticity for performing an initially new behaviour (that is, performing an action automatically). They found that it takes on average 66 days (not 21!) to develop a new habit, with people often taking beyond 230 days of repetition to change habits long-term.

As adults, the goal should not be just to simply get better at doing more of the same. The type of learning that makes a difference consists specifically of new, novel challenges.

Elkhonon Goldberg, 2013 [21]

Neurons wire together if they fire together.

Hebb's Rule [22]

Remember, we've got to overcome the old habits and routines to create the new ones: the brain needs constant reminders and time to reorganise neural pathways based on new experiences.

Our neurons are responsible for everything we do (together with our nervous systems). Neurons link up with each other and form strong bonds based on our experiences, emotions, thoughts, and interactions with the environment. [23,24]

Think of it like this: have you ever heard a piece of music that triggers memories of a certain time in your life? Or had sudden memories, triggered by a particular person, clothing, smells or sensations? When this happens, it is because of this neural wiring.

When music or other sensations activates one area of your brain, electrical impulses cascade to the surrounding neurons. The pathways that were created when you first had that experience allow the memories to be re-triggered.

Remember, the term 'neuroplasticity' refers to the lifelong ability of the brain to reorganise neural pathways based on new experiences.[25,26] This means we can actually rewire our brain by choosing what we expose ourselves to. This is why habits are possible to break.

When we think of our habits, we often think of the ones that are not good for us - smoking, not exercising, unhealthy eating, gambling, checking and rechecking emails or social media pages, to name a few.

But remember, a habit is also anything you do as a matter of routine. And the longer you have been doing something a certain way, the harder that habit is to break. Even if you make some attempt to change your behaviour, it is very easy to find yourself back in an unwanted behavioural pattern. This is due to the strength of those neural connections in the brain.

At MIT, the researcher Catherine Thorn and her colleagues identified areas located within the brain that account for these connections and habit formation: the basal ganglia. The basal ganglia are a collection of nuclei found on both sides of the thalamus, outside and above the limbic system, (which is one of the oldest parts of the brain), but below the cingulate gyrus and within the temporal lobes.

The basal ganglia play a large role in movement control, emotion, cognition, and reward-based learning. Within the basal ganglia, there are two areas responsible for the functions that work in unison to form habits. The main component of the basal ganglia – as defined functionally - is the striatum (**Figure 1**), which comprises:

1. The **dorsolateral** part of the striatum controls movement and is connected to sensorimotor functioning (seeing, hearing, moving, etc.). When we move a part of our body in a new way and it feels good, this area is active.

2. The **dorsomedial** striatum controls flexible behaviour and is connected to areas where associations are recognised and formed. When we feel a sense of accomplishment for having tried something new, the association is recognised here. Our brain then experiences reinforcement (formation beginning) that this new activity is one that serves us well.

Repetition of actions and behaviours impacts on the striatum to create new habits. Hence **a habit is when you've done something so many times that your body knows how to do it better than your mind**.

A protein blend, collectively known as myelin, insulates the wiring between the neurons (Morell & Quarles, 1999). Every time you repeat an action or a thought, the neuron fires faster, and the more easily it fires, the thicker and denser the myelin coating becomes. This makes the pathways stronger, and the habit becomes more ingrained.

This is what is going on in our brains when we are learning something

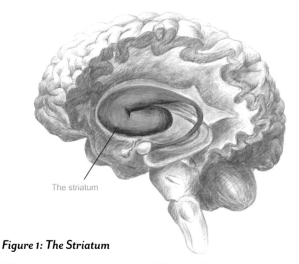

The striatum

Figure 1: The Striatum

The brain does not know the difference between the habits that serve us well and those that don't serve us well, and this is why we often create unhealthy habits.

new. And it's helpful for you as an adult learner to understand what it will take to create new neural pathways, so that you can more consciously make an effort to repeat the action until it becomes habit. In my experience, just knowing that it may take over two months and potentially a lot more than that to create a new habit helps me to set more realistic targets for myself and the people I work with. It also helps me to not give myself a hard time when I 'fall off the wagon'!

Accept that it may take longer than you think to embed the new learning and to create or change a habit. Just because you stop the new behaviour does not mean you are unable to form this new habit. It just means that it is challenging for you because the existing neurons are linked strongly to each other based on repetition. Perseverance will, in time, create even stronger pathways and connections to reinforce your new habit.

The great news is that bursts of doing your new activity strengthen the connections between the neurons each and every time!

Even if it takes 21 days, or 66 days or even beyond 230 days to become automatic, the hard work to change a given habit will surely be worth the effort. Eventually you will find yourself automatically having those difficult conversations in a calmer way, or taking thinking time to plan strategically, or delegating like a true leader. When you notice the learning has bedded down, and the new way of operating has become habit, you will have a real sense of achievement, and looking back at how you used to do things and how you used to feel, you will possibly feel relieved!

The Brain's Protection Mode

The prefrontal cortex (PFC) occupies one-third of the entire human cerebral cortex and is dedicated to sustaining rapid computations required to accomplish a wide range of mental activities. The PFC is also connected to our limbic system, where our emotions and memories are housed. But the processing of the interaction between the PFC and the limbic system happens unconsciously, and so we are not aware of how our memories, our emotions, and how our deeply held beliefs rule how we make decisions and how we problem-solve.

When you want to make a change in how you operate, you need to consider the brain's urge to protect you. When you start to think about doing something a different way and you start to believe that this change is possible, your left prefrontal cortex (LPFC) – the area of the brain above your left eye – will focus on getting that done. However, very quickly, fear of failure or fear of the unknown can activate the fear centre of your brain: the amygdala.

The amygdala is a small almond-shaped structure that sits directly in front of the hippocampus, in the limbic system (the more primitive parts of the brain) in each hemisphere. It has a particular role in emotions and memories.

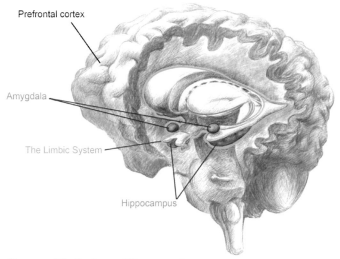

Figure 2: The Prefrontal Cortex and
The Limbic System including Amygdala and Hippocampus

When you start to do something a different way, the brain works out very quickly that you are disturbing its homeostasis. Blood flows towards the older areas of the brain, and the amygdala sets off a whole lot of sequences that put your brain and body into fight, flight or freeze. This makes it challenging for the LPFC to keep focused on achieving the outcome you want because the blood is flowing away from it towards the more primitive parts of the brain. You could say that the more ancient parts of your brain are rebelling against what you want to do. This happens because the brain is focused on working as efficiently as it can to keep you safe. And the amygdala experiences a change in habit as dangerous.

To make real lasting change, you will have to manage your amygdala and manage your emotions. For example, with the fear of failure, the difficult part is that you may not even be conscious of that fear. Our brain's subconscious operating system runs automatically and focuses on retaining energy and protecting us from any harm or discomfort. So, when our brain tells us that 'change' is a harmful experience, we almost have to be ahead of it, to be able to fool it, if we are going to make a change. That's why I mentioned earlier that learning and change requires getting to know yourself better.

CHAPTER THREE:

Overcoming the Brain's Protection Mode and Creating Supportive Habits

As stated in the **Introduction**, the objective of this book is to give you an understanding of the brain, learning and habit change as a fundamental mechanism to learning. This section suggests strategies to overcome the brain's self-protection mode that will help you make learning happen in a much more effective way. If you are in a supportive role to other people's learning, it is important to seriously consider how you can implement this information into each person's learning journey and therefore I provide some tips and exercises that can be used to do so.

Improve your Self-Talk and Focus on the Possibilities and the Positives and Get Curious

Ever given a presentation and found yourself berating yourself during or after it? Your thoughts go something like "the audience think I don't know what I'm talking about", or "the audience look bored", or "I am terrible at giving presentations". Afterwards, one of your colleagues mentions you did a great job. You berate yourself for giving yourself a hard time.

Pay attention to the negative stories, the disempowering beliefs you are telling yourself. Your mind is constantly creating opinions for you and making decisions for you that you are perhaps not even aware of.

Our thinking, conscious and unconscious, rules our behaviour. And most of the decisions we make are based on the stories we tell ourselves. Most of these stories we are repeating, over and over and over again. There is also 'unconscious thinking': all sorts of unconscious cognitive processes taking place that we are not necessarily aware of, and that are driving our behaviours. Two of the most famous modern psychologists and Nobel prize winners, Kahneman and Tversky, conducted decades of research on this topic. The particular beliefs, biases or stories we have about ourselves, conscious and unconscious, we have on a daily basis are thousands, and are all controlling how we operate in life.

As discussed above, the memories and emotions housed in the ancient parts of your brain are managing your behaviours and decisions, even though we like to think it is the newer cognitive processes that are at the helm of our actions.

I've been working with clients for over 10 years and I see time and time again the power that our beliefs and our stories have over our own learning success. Some of the thoughts that people share with me have included: "I'm not good enough", "I don't belong", "What if they think I am stupid?". Of course, there are others who believe the story "I'm better than everyone" - and this can also block learning and habit change!

Many of the stories we believe about ourselves have come from people outside of ourselves. What are the messages you have received since you were young from family, friends, teachers, and colleagues? For example: "You're not as clever as your brother", "You'll never amount to anything", "You're weird", "You're not a natural leader". Pay attention to these stories and consciously start changing them. It's time to focus on getting your beliefs and your emotions congruent with the healthier, more positive habits you want to create.

If you can improve your self-talk with these beliefs and stories, you can change brain blood flow. This will increase the natural chemicals that help you feel relaxed (opiods) and activate your reward (dopamine) pathways. The increased amounts of these chemicals can help you feel more motivated - and this is one of the important steps to positive change.

I invite you to consider an area of your life you would like to improve or change and do the following:

1. Write any thought / belief / story you have in your head that is not supportive of you in this specific area of your life.

2. To the right of the first list, write a list of any evidence you can possibly think of that proves those initial thoughts to be incorrect.

3. To the right of the second list, write yourself a list of more supportive thoughts you could choose to have about yourself.

4. To the right of the third list, write a list of questions you could ask yourself anytime you find yourself thinking the unsupportive thoughts. The questions ideally are focused on the positive rather than the negative. The questions will engage your LPFC and take the focus away from your amygdala.

You will now have a list of four columns. Then:

1. Save the third and fourth columns - the list of more supportive thoughts and the list of questions - in your reminders on your phone to remind you daily.

2. Write these columns on Post-its to stick on a wall / computer / notebook - somewhere you will see them every day.

In a sense, you are going to 'brainwash' your brain to believe these more supportive beliefs. So that you can manage your emotions, In doing so you can manage your amygdala.

For example: Kay was asked to deliver a presentation and she was dreading it. (see table on next page)

The problem is that it's easier to fill ourselves with and focus on negative emotions, because they are stronger and they keep us safe. Our brain's focus on self-protection means negative emotions have a stronger hold on us. Negative emotions are much more attention-grabbing and intense and so they linger longer than positive emotions. But we need to try hard to focus on positive emotions. Because research has found that when we experience positive emotions, we see more possibility. When we see the possibilities, this helps the LPFC to keep focused on the task and the plan.

Thought / Belief / Story	Evidence Against	Empowering & Supportive Belief	Questions
"What if they think I am stupid?"	I was invited to interview	I am smart	What great things can transpire from me presenting?
	I got the job	I am capable	
	My manager regularly asks for my input on projects	I am an expert	
		I am clever	
		I am passionate about this area	What interesting questions will people ask me?
	I passed all my exams	I love sharing information with other people	
	I was invited to deliver this presentation because I know what I am talking about	The information I have to share is interesting	What good conversations will follow this presentation?
		When people ask challenging questions, I can report back to them later	
	I have read everything I can about this topic		What will I learn in the process?

Therefore, it is vital to focus on the possibilities of why you CAN rather than why you won't or can't.

The challenge of living in a questioning mode:

So many of the choices and decisions we make, and the habits we have that don't serve us, come from not asking enough questions and not being curious about options and alternatives.

It's challenging for many adults to live in a questioning, curious frame of mind. Many of us like to make statements to ourselves and others. It makes us feel secure. It helps us feel like we have control. It shows that we know what we are talking about. At least, we think it does!

As mentioned above, when you start to think about doing something a different way and you start to believe that this change is possible, your LPFC will focus on getting that done. But fear of failure or fear of the unknown can activate the fear centre of your brain: the amygdala.

Ask yourself "When I take action what new things will I learn and what new things will I experience, regardless of the outcome?". When challenges arise, ask yourself "What is possible when I break through?". If you can get curious, you will re-engage your LPFC and override your amygdala and its inducement of fear.

Please remember what I said earlier, much of our fear is unconscious and it takes a lot of self-awareness to recognise this fear.

Experiment with 'Habit Loops'

MIT researchers discovered a pattern they named 'habit loops'. These loops consist of three parts:

* A cue (that causes or starts the behaviour).

* A routine (the behaviour you want to change).

* A reward (the benefit you get from that behaviour).

For example, sitting at your desk you may feel bored (a cue); you check email (a routine); you get momentary distraction from boredom (a reward). But when this reward wears off, the loop continues. You feel bored again at your desk (a cue); you check email (a routine), etc. Thus, the habit has been created.

We all have different cues that initiate the habit loop. For one person the cue might be boredom, for another feeling lonely at your desk, and for someone else, it's disliking their work. You need to get to know your cues. Only you will know what your cues are, and clarity on this will come through experimentation.

For example, Tom was a very effective employee and the company that had recently acquired the business he worked with needed him to document a huge range of processes that were in his head that kept his section of the business running smoothly (reward).

One of the reasons I was asked to work with Tom was that he had become very stressed and his stress was being expressed in, for example, in his 'snappy responses' to his team.

On reflection, Tom particularly noticed that when he arrived at the office every morning, he felt stressed (routine).

He spent some time over the course of a few weeks trying to figure out his cue for this routine of stress: Was it when his alarm went off in the morning? Was it the traffic on the way to the office? Was it the face of a particular person he had to walk by to get to his desk? Nope, it turned out it was an in-tray on his desk, which was the first thing he would see every morning when he walked towards his desk. As soon as he removed that in-tray (cue) from his line of sight, he noticed that he stopped going into his habit of feeling stressed (routine) and his mornings at work felt more relaxed (reward) at the outset of his days! Starting his days feeling less stressed impacted positively on the rest of the day as he felt more in control of how he felt. This impacted positively on the people around him. Seems so simple, doesn't it? Often changing the cue can change everything!

As you get to know your cues and the rewards that come from your routines, you can get more awareness of, and control over, your habits. This is a vital step in overcoming the brain's self-protection mode. Start exploring and experimenting with the loops that exist in your habits so that you override the habits stored in your basal ganglia.

Match in with your Personal Values

Values are the things that you believe are important in the way you live and work. Posner [27] defines a value as being something that an individual will make a sacrifice to obtain; a belief upon which a person acts by preference; or an enduring belief that a specific mode of conduct is personally or socially preferable.

Just a few examples of values we are living by but do not necessarily consciously think about in how we go about our days are: accomplishment, agility, boldness, calmness, health, honesty, integrity, learning, love, playfulness, passion, purposefulness, respect, reliability, rigor .... the list goes on and on.

How can getting congruent with your values help you make habit change?

I find that the 'ah-ha' moments that people have, come when they start to recognise the decisions they are making in their own lives based on values that they either took for granted, or had never named. And it is often a mind-blowing moment.

This is because, generally, we take our values for granted and don't really think about them.

I remember the first time I did a coaching exercise to work out my own personal values, approximately 10 years ago. Listing out the values that were important to me, I realised my top value was 'freedom'. Suddenly, all the decisions I had been making in my life up to that point made sense. I was being driven by my value of freedom, but it wasn't necessarily getting me to where I wanted to be in my career and relationships. I had to become more conscious of the decisions I was making around this top value and question myself as to whether this was the value that I wanted to live to or if it was someone else's value that had been passed on to me.

Who created or owns your values? Our values arise from our beliefs. Many of our beliefs come from our society, our parents, our peers. And therefore, some of your values might not consciously have been chosen by you personally. It's therefore important to get clarity on your own values and ask yourself if YOU have CHOSEN them, or if they have been passed on to you by others. If we are living our parents' values (which many of us are, unbeknownst to ourselves), we are potentially going to make decisions, consciously and unconsciously, that are not what we actually want for ourselves in life. It may appear on the outside that you are doing the right thing with your life, career and family, but for who and from who's perspective?

I recommend writing a list of your top 10 values in no particular order. Then reorganise the list in order of importance to you, from most important to least important. Identify your top 3 from this ordered list of 10, and ask yourself: "Are these values bringing me where I want to be in my life?". Then, ask "If I lived in an alternative universe, and I could only take these top 3 with me, would they definitely be the ones I would take (knowing I have to leave the other 7 behind)?". If you are happy that they are the top 3 values that are most important to you, ask yourself: "Am I truly living to these top 3 values, in how I spend my time, and the decisions I make in life and work?" and then "Do I need to reorder these values and make decisions, prioritising certain values over others?".

This exercise might help you realise that you wish to reorder your values. It will then help you start prioritising what / who with / where you spend your time, and start making some decisions differently as to how you want to live and what you might need to change.

For example, after working through this exercise to get clarity on personal values, one of my clients confirmed that his top values were health, belonging, and success. But on exploring how and if he was living to these values, he admitted that he was working a 14-hour day, was not feeling healthy at all, and was not spending the time he would like with his family. Therefore, his values of belonging and health were not being lived by him.

He was what we might call successful in his career as he was a manager, pipped to become part of the senior leadership team. But not all of the senior management team saw him as a good 'fit'. Becoming part of the senior leadership team was going to involve him making changes to how he communicated and delegated, so although he was living to his value of success, there were a few personal obstacles in the way to him being as successful as he wished to be. Regarding health and belonging, although he had been trying to cut down his working hours for years, he had failed for one reason or another, and was not doing any exercise, was eating mostly fast food and spending limited time with family and none with friends.

By re-focusing on the values that were most important to him over the course of one year, in how he actually wished to live his life, he re-arranged how he was operating. He consciously chose to spend more time with his family and friends and put a fitness regime in place. He also committed to changing his habits of not delegating, and he learned new ways to communicate. He had to change many ingrained habits. He had to change how he communicated, and how he behaved with his colleagues in many ways. He had to delegate to others, speak up more in meetings and adopt new body language. But by getting clarity on what was most important to him and making decisions based on these values he found clarity and the discipline to change, and he made it on to the senior leadership team. The initial opportunity and motivation to change how he operated came from the chance of promotion. This motivated him to work with me as his coach. But it was getting clarity on, and alignment with, his values that helped him to find the discipline to change his habitual routines.

We won't make ourselves more creative and productive by copying other people's habits, even the habits of geniuses; we must know our own nature, and what habits serve us best.

Gretchen Rubin, 2015 [28]

Consider the Four Tendencies

I mentioned earlier that motivation to do things differently is short-lived. It is discipline that creates the habit. In Gretchen Rubin's book *The Four Tendencies, 2017,* she discusses how each of us fall into one of four categories in how we approach life and how we respond to expectations; our own and others. Knowing that motivation will only last so long, it is useful to consider these four tendencies, because it provides insight into what you might need to put in place to keep the discipline going long enough to create the new habit. Rubin names these four tendencies as:

* Upholders.

* Questioners.

* Obligers.

* Rebels.

Considering which category we fall into MOST of the time can be very useful in considering how we approach learning and habit change.

Upholders ("Discipline is my freedom")
When it comes to changing habits, upholders generally meet both inner and outer expectations, meaning they don't want to let others or themselves down. They are self-directed, and take initiative without supervision but they hate to do things wrong and put a high value on follow-through. They have a strong instinct for self-preservation and benefit from scheduling classes or meetings to ensure they follow-through on changing habits and learning.

Questioners ("I'll Comply- If You Convince Me Why")
Questioners meet only inner expectations. They push back against and question all expectations. Above all, they do something only if they think it makes sense – they hate anything arbitrary. They must

understand the science, the facts and purpose before they will make the time and effort to do something differently.

Obligers ("You can count on me")

Obligers meet outer expectations but not always inner ones. In other words, they usually need some form of external accountability: a coach, supervisor, manager or accountability partner! They put a high value on meeting commitments to others. They have trouble delegating and often feel they must do everything themselves. But if Obligers feel taken advantage of, where they are giving all the time to others, they will rebel.

Rebels ("You can't make me, and neither can I")

Rebels resist both inner and outer expectations. Often the mere fact that someone wants them to do something will make them want to refuse. They take pleasure in defying other people. They value authenticity, freedom, self-expression and spontaneity. Rebels do better when there are no expectations at all. If a Rebel wants to do something differently, they need to consider how this ties in with their identity: "Of course I am going to do this thing, this is who I am!". The Rebel needs to understand the information to be able to make an informed decision, the consequences of actions they might take and be able to make their own choices. The more we interfere with a Rebel, the more they will resist. [29]

Taking Rubin's online Four Tendencies questionnaire to work out which tendency you have may help you work out what course of action you need to take to change how you do things. If you are an Obliger or an Upholder, for example, you definitely need someone else to keep you accountable on the changes you wish to make and the learnings you wish to apply.

Consider the Obstacles

What tangible obstacles will get in your way? Deciding what you want to achieve is not enough to make real change occur. Otherwise it would be simple to learn new skills and to change our habits. You must get clear on the obstacles that will get in the way of you making change. As well as managing the obstacles we have discussed in your own brain, you need to consider the obstacles in the material world that will get in the way.

For example, as mentioned earlier, Kay had to learn to delegate more of her work to her team. She recognised that she needed to do this for her own health and well-being as since taking over this new team, she was working very long hours and often working at weekends. She also knew she needed to empower her team to learn and grow. But the obstacles were many. She had psychological obstacles. Her beliefs included "My team will be annoyed with me as they already have enough to do"; "I will be the cause of my team's stress"; and "My team won't think I am a good manager". She believed that her role was to nurture her team, and that doing a lot of this work for them meant she was nurturing them. There were also plenty of physical obstacles such as working in an office separate to her team. For her, this meant that sometimes when an individual sent her a document, it was quicker to make corrections to it herself than find that person to have a quick conversation about necessary changes.

If you can become conscious of your obstacles, it will help your brain to avoid moving into protection mode – telling yourself rational lies as to why you are better off doing things the way you have always done them, when you meet obstacles. Get clear on the obstacles that will get in your way upfront, so that you can arm yourself to overcome them!

Here's a writing exercise you could perform on this:

* List out all obstacles in the way of completing your goal.

* Identify the largest obstacles.

* Clearly visualise those obstacles. What do those obstacles look, sound and feel like?

* What will you do to overcome those obstacles?

By bringing the obstacles that we all know are there somewhere into our conscious experience, we are more likely to make the change. This is called Mental Contrasting. In many of the studies in which mental contrasting was tested, participants were instructed to use the technique just once – taking just a few minutes. Afterwards, changes in behaviour were observed for up to several weeks.

Make Learning and Habit Change Enjoyable

Think of a time you really enjoyed learning something. What were you doing? Who were you with? When you enjoyed it, learning came as second nature.
Think back to when you were a child.
If you send a child to piano lessons and she doesn't like learning the piano, it is highly unlikely that she will learn anything past what is set by her teacher for exams. On the other hand, if the child has begged to attend piano lessons and she really wants to learn, the chances are she will progress quickly and happily and gain joy from the process, even when the work is challenging. Because this activity started with passion, she created good practice habits, and her knowledge and enthusiasm is more likely to remain with her for years to come, perhaps for her whole life. What is followed in interest or fun is more likely to create more interest and fun.

The degree to which you retain your mental faculties depends on a number of simple behavioural factors...The more you learn, the more you can learn. We know that new learning can have profound physiological effects on the brain.

Ian Robertson, 2005 [32]

As children, we learned by playing, making up stories, creating games together and actively using our imagination. Believe it or not, this is how we best learn as adults; when learning is engaging, fun, and full of "imagining the possibilities".

Experts and researchers [30,31] all over the world have found that brains grow best in the context of interactive discovery and through the co-creation of stories that shape and support memories of what is being learned.

Learning together in groups, with communities and friends or in our teams has many benefits and creates long-term impact, partly because it creates accountability.

What could you do to make learning more enjoyable for yourself, and to connect with your purpose, passion and values? For example, will having a friend accompany you to an exercise class every second day make it easier to get there, because it will be fun to do it together? Will working with a colleague or a coach to manage your team more effectively make you more accountable in making the change? Would considering that if your purpose was to become more effective at empowering your colleagues, in order to create a happier working environment, because you are aware of all the research on happy work environments and productivity, help you feel like you have a worthy cause?

If you are having fun, enjoying yourself and feeling psychologically safe, you will again manage to avoid an amygdala hijack!

Recognise the Importance of Learning for the Longevity of Your Memory

If you are not getting all that excited at this point about the 'Learning Brain', you might also think about this: like any part of the body, the brain will degrade as we get older. To help keep the brain healthy, we want to stimulate it with new types of learning to keep creating new pathways.

Doidge states that the way to stave off memory loss into old age is to keep learning new things.

... learning new physical activities that require concentration, solving challenging puzzles, or making a career change that requires that you master new skills and materials.

Norman Doidge, 2007[33]

I believe it is important to develop and maintain an appetite for learning regardless of your age, and in every area of your life. We can never know enough. To keep up with the pace of change in the world and to keep our brain younger for longer, it's good to stay hungry for learning. There is always a new musical instrument or another language. Or a new team to learn from.

Norman Doidge's book *The Brain that Changes Itself* [33] is a truly inspiring collection of studies, real-life examples and conclusions on the plasticity of the brain. It tells of how the brain can reorganise itself and make new neural connections throughout life. Unlike what we once believed about the brain – that it is hardwired and wears out with age – these stories show that the brain is at your disposal to use and grow to YOUR benefit, and to promote mental longevity. I recommend reading this book as it will inspire you to get focused on challenging your brain and learning new things. Doidge states that the way to stave off memory loss into old age is to keep learning new things.

... learning new physical activities that require concentration, solving challenging puzzles, or making a career change that requires that you master new skills and materials.
Norman Doidge, 2007 [33]

Key Take-Aways

Now you have a good picture of why learning in adulthood can be challenging compared to when you were a child. Knowing that change is possible if you give focus to replacing old habits, and repeating to allow the new neural pathways to be created and consolidated, will help you get there. To summarise:

To stay one step ahead of your brain's protection mode:

* Improve your self-talk: pay attention to the stories, and the disempowering beliefs.

* Focus on CAN, rather than can't or won't.

* Keep curious rather than berating yourself or giving up.

* Experiment with habit loops: a routine (the behaviour you want to change), a cue (that causes or starts the behaviour) and a reward (the benefit you get from that behaviour).

* Match in with your values, the things that are most important to you in the way you live and work.

* Consider which of the Four Tendencies you are: Upholder, Questioner, Obliger, or Rebel.

* Consider if working with someone to achieving your goals or having someone hold you accountable to your plan of action will help you get there.

* Consider the obstacles that are sure to transpire and be ready for them.

* Use childhood tools of imagination, curiosity and fun to make content memorable and change enjoyable.

* Recognise the importance of learning for the longevity of your memory.

In the past 10 years of working with individuals, groups and teams, the greatest successes have come from people understanding the information presented in this book as a foundation to their learning and habit change. It's a cliché to say, but it's true, the people whose learning and change I have facilitated have been my best teachers. In the coming days and weeks, you will find yourself noticing your own habits, your own approach to learning and your brain's protection mode.

There is also a process and structure that I have noticed which, when implemented into a person's or a group's learning, creates a more personal connection with the knowledge being shared and therefore assists long-term behavioural change. You will find this in another book in the **Maximising Brain Potential** series: **Developing Learning Addicts: The 7 Steps To Learning & Habit Change**.

Notes

1   Peter Drucker, Austrian-born American management consultant: quote 56: https://succeedfeed.com/peter-drucker-quotes/

2   Alvin Toffler, American writer and businessman: https://www.goodreads.com/author/quotes/3030.Alvin_Toffler

3   Duhigg, C. (2013). New York Times Best-Selling Author of Smarter Faster Better and The Power of Habit, 12 February, charlesduhigg.com/.

4   Graybiel, A. (2008). 'Habits, Rituals, and the Evaluative Brain', Annual Review of Neuroscience, 31, pp.359-387.

5   Vinvent Van Gogh, famous Dutch painter : https://www.goodreads.com/author/quotes/34583.Vincent_van_Gogh

6   Merzenich, M. How You Can Make Your Brain Smarter Every Day, 6 Aug. 2013, www.forbes.com/sites/nextavenue/2013/08/06/how-you-can-make-your-brain-smarter-every-day/#2550a35334ef.

7   Cozolino, L. and Sprokay, S. (2006). 'Neuroscience and Adult Learning', New Directions for Adult and Continuing Education, Summer 2006 (110), pp. 11-19.

8   Buonomano, D.V. and Merzenich, M.M. (1998). 'Cortical Plasticity: From Synapses to Maps', Annual Review of Neuroscience, 21(1), pp. 149-186.

9   Trojan, S. and Pokorny, J. (1999). 'Theoretical Aspects of Neuroplasticity', Physiological Research, 48(2), pp. 87-97.

10 Guzowski, J.F., Setlow, B., Wagner, E.K. and McGaugh, J.L. (2001). Experience-dependent Gene Expression in the Rat Hippocampus After Spatial Learning: A Comparison of the Immediate-early Genes Arc, c-fos, and zif268', Journal of Neuroscience, 21(14), pp. 5089-5098.

11 Ickes, B.R., Pham, T.M., Sanders, L.A., Albeck, D.S., Mohammed, A.H. and Granholm, A.C. (2000). 'Long-term Environmental Enrichment Leads to Regional Increases in Neurotrophin Levels in Rat Brain', Experimental Neurology, 164, pp. 45-52.

12 Kempermann, G., Kuhn, H.G. and Gage, F.H. (1998). Experience-induced Neurogenesis in the Senescent Dentate Gyrus', Journal of Neuroscience, 18(9), pp. 3206-3212.

13 Kolb, B. and Whishaw, I.Q. (1998). 'Brain Plasticity and Behaviour', Annual Review of Psychology, 49, pp. 43-64.

14 Kolb. B. and Gibb, R. (2011). 'Brain Plasticity and Behaviour in the Developing Brain', Journal of the Canadian Academy of Child & Adolescent Psychiatry, 20(4): 265–276.

15 Altman, J., Wallace, R.B., Anderson, W.J. and Das, G.D. (1968). 'Behaviourally Induced Changes in Length of Cerebrum in Rats', Developmental Psychology, 1(2), pp. 112-117.

16 Kolb. B. and Gibb, R. (1991). 'Environmental Enrichment and Cortical Injury: Behavioural and Anatomical Consequences of Frontal Cortex Lesions', Cerebral Cortex, 1(2), pp. 189-198.

17 Schrott, L.M., Denenberg, V.H., Sherman, G.F., Waters, N.S., Rosen, G.D. and Galaburda, A.M. (1992). 'Environmental Enrichment, Neocortical Ectopias, and Behaviour in the Autoimmune NZB mouse', Developmental Brain Research, 67(1), pp. 85-93.

18 Schrott, L.M. (1997). 'Effect of Training and Environment on Brain Morphology and Behaviour', Acta Paediatrica, 86 (S422), pp. 45-47.

19   Kolb. B. and Gibb, R. (2011). 'Brain Plasticity and Behaviour in the Developing Brain', Journal of the Canadian Academy of Child & Adolescent Psychiatry, 20(4): 265–276.

20   Cozolino, L. and Sprokay, S. (2006). 'Neuroscience and Adult Learning', New Directions for Adult and Continuing Education, Summer 2006 (110), pp. 11-19.

21   Goldberg, E. (2013). The Sharpbrains Guide to Brain Fitness: How to Optimize Brain Health and Performance at Any Age, Sharpbrains, Inc.

22   Donald Olding Hebb, Canadian psychologist - Hebb's Rule : https://neuroquotient.com/en/pshychology-and-neuroscience-hebb-principle-rule/

23   Buonomano, D.V. and Merzenich, M.M. (1998). 'Cortical Plasticity: From Synapses to Maps', Annual Review of Neuroscience, 21(1), pp. 149-186.

24   Trojan, S. and Pokorny, J. (1999). 'Theoretical Aspects of Neuroplasticity', Physiological Research, 48(2), pp. 87-97.

25   Buonomano, D.V. and Merzenich, M.M. (1998). 'Cortical Plasticity: From Synapses to Maps', Annual Review of Neuroscience, 21(1), pp. 149-186

26   Trojan, S. and Pokorny, J. (1999). 'Theoretical Aspects of Neuroplasticity', Physiological Research, 48(2), pp. 87-97.

27   Posner, B.Z. and Munson, J.M. (1979). 'The Importance of Values in Understanding Organisational Behaviour, Human Resource Management, 18(3): 9-14.

28   Rubin, G. (2015). Better Than Before: What I Learned About Making and Breaking Habits – to Sleep More, Quit Sugar, Procrastinate Less, and Generally Build a Happier Life, Hodder.

29 Rubin, G. (2017). The Four Tendencies: The Indispensable Personality Profiles that Reveal How to Make Your Life Better (and Other People's Lives Better, Too), London: Two Roads, an imprint of John Murray Press.

30 Cozolino, L. and Sprokay, S. (2006). 'Neuroscience and Adult Learning', New Directions for Adult and Continuing Education, Summer 2006 (110), pp. 11-19.

31 Caine, R.N. and Caine, G. (1990). Understanding a Brain-based Approach to Learning and Teaching', Educational Leadership, 48(2), pp. 66-70.

32 Burns, V. (2005). Keep Your Brain Sharp with the Magnificent Seven Tips, 8 September, https://www.irishtimes.com/news/keep-your-brain-sharp-with-the-magnificent-seven-tips-1.489543.

33 Doidge, N. (2007). The Brain that Changes Itself, New York: Viking Press

Adaptas

Adaptas consists of a team of experts with a range of backgrounds, combined to impact personal and organisational change. Working with individuals, groups and teams in organisations internationally, we have a strong focus on narrowing the gap between learning and the real world, and on linking development with outcomes in a way that is effective and lasting. This approach brings people on a truly unique and engaging experience of learning, enabling them to be more effective and impactful in their roles.

Popular topics include:

* Leadership Development: Leading Self and Leading Others.

* Creating and Maintaining High Performing Teams.

* Maximising Brain Potential to Manage Change.

* Developing Emotional Intelligence.

* Unconscious Bias, Diversity and Inclusion.

* Communication: Influencing, Difficult & Coaching Conversations & Presentations.

* Negotiation – Understanding your Thinking and Behaviour to avoid a 'one style fits all approach'.

* Creating and Maintaining a Happier and More Accountable Culture: Values & Behaviours.

* Improvisation in Business for an Ever-Changing World.

* Resilience, Stress Management and Mental Toughness.

* Brain Management: Cultivate the brain's potential for productivity, creativity and peace.

Adaptas has been an early adopter of new technologies that bring an added layer of immersion to learning in organisations. These include Virtual Reality and Augmented Reality learning solutions.

Oak Tree Press

Oak Tree Press develops and delivers information, advice and resources for entrepreneurs and managers. It is Ireland's leading business book publisher, with an unrivalled reputation for quality titles across business, management, HR, law, marketing and enterprise topics.

Oak Tree Press is comfortable across a range of communication media - print, web and training, focusing always on the effective communication of business information.

Oak Tree Press

E: info@oaktreepress.com

W: www.oaktreepress.com / www.SuccessStore.com.